COUNTRY
PAINTING
·PROJECTS·

COUNTRY
PAINTING
·PROJECTS·

decorating on wood, pottery and metal

EMMA HUNK

David & Charles

A DAVID & CHARLES BOOK

First published in the UK in 1996
Reprinted 1997, 1998

A catalogue record for this book is available from the British Library.

ISBN 0 7153 0342 2

Book design by Diana Knapp
Photography by Shona Wood
Printed in Italy by New Interlitho SpA
for David & Charles
Brunel House Newton Abbot Devon

CONTENTS

INTRODUCTION

During the mid-1980s, I lived in the United States and I was continually intrigued by the painted crafts and accessories on display and available throughout the country. Muted and apparently antique colours were combined with charming naive motifs, stencilled onto everything from Shaker boxes to dressers. I had always had an interest in arts and crafts but had no formal training and lacked sufficient confidence in my abilities. I would admire many of the items and, like so many others, think 'I could do that...'. But, again like so many others, I never found the time to try, persuading myself that there must be some secret ingredient that I didn't know about. Anyway, how much safer to think that you could do it but never find the time to try (and risk possible failure!).

Almost a decade later, I have become a painting addict. As soon as I first saw a demonstration of a simple stencilling technique and realized that I really could do it, I was hooked. A friend then gave me a crash course in decorative painting techniques and from that moment on, nothing in our house was safe from the paintbrush. I soon learnt just how wonderful a stencil is in the way that it enabled me to produce consistently professional designs (initially thanks to the clever stencil designers and manufacturers). Practice with the stencils and stencil paints soon led me into simple shading and highlighting techniques, transforming a flat design into something that is three-dimensional and alive.

I very much hope that this book will help to release the artist trapped inside you. I don't know how many times I've overheard people looking at my work and saying, 'It's very nice, but I could never do that'. I'm sure that they could and this book aims to show you how to paint a simple household item and turn it into something that you can be proud of.

I have tried to make the designs and techniques as simple and straightforward as possible and the items suggested to paint are inexpensive. There are some pieces of equipment and artist's materials that I do highly recommend for the projects and some of these can seem expensive, especially when purchased together. If taken care of, however, the equipment that you buy will last a long time and give you a great deal of pleasure and satisfaction.

Happy painting!

OPPOSITE   To make any of the objects in this book
you require only a minimal amount of materials.

MATERIALS &

MATERIALS AND PAINTS

When you are painting your chosen object, you will find a few other materials useful in addition to the items listed below. Always have a few clean, soft rags to hand to clean up inadvertent spillages of paint or water, or runs and drips on the background. Some small white saucers or plates for mixing paints are also useful.

BRUSHES

To create any of the designs that feature in this book, you will need only a few paintbrushes. For backgrounds, I suggest that you use a good quality 1½in (3.5cm) wide flat paintbrush. The better the quality, the less likely you are to have stray bristles falling out of the brush and getting stuck in your meticulously executed paintwork.

For applying the motifs through a stencil, use a stencil brush. You can purchase these from most craft shops and look for one that is approximately ½in (12mm) wide as this is the most adaptable for whatever the size of the stencil. Then, for the detail work, I recommend just three sizes of artist's paintbrush – Nos. 1, 4 and 6. Armed with these three brushes, you will be able to paint detailed and larger areas of colour equally well.

When cleaning your paintbrushes, make sure that you do a very thorough job so that the next time you

TECHNIQUES

come to use them, they will be as good as new. A meticulous clean will also mean that the last colour you used won't inadvertently appear when the brush is next used. For brushes that have been used in oil-based paints, massage some white spirit into the bristles to get rid of all the oily residue. Those that have been used with water-based paints need only be washed in some detergent, such as washing-up liquid, and then rinsed thoroughly in tap water.

PAINTS

For most backgrounds I suggest that you use a mid-sheen oil-based paint. Don't use a gloss paint as the resultant surface is too shiny for applying acrylics onto with ease. However, the hard surface created by an oil-based paint is ideal for drawing onto in chalks or pencils and the end result is more durable.

When painting the motifs, I tend to use acrylic paints. Being water-based, these are easy to mix to make beautifully subtle shades. Emulsion paints are just as good and indeed, you can mix acrylics and emulsions together, should you need to. Of course, you could also paint the motifs using oil paints or even enamel paints, but they do take a long time to dry and so completing an image would take much longer than using a water-based colour. Likewise, poster paints could be used, but they can be very thin and the colours produced aren't as subtle as acrylics or emulsion paints.

Painting materials (starting top left and working in an anti-clockwise direction): artist's paintbrushes, stencil paintbrushes, oil and acrylic paints, flat paintbrush, chalk, pencils, varnish.

Several of the projects in this book feature gold paint. After much experimenting, I have found that an oil-based gold is the best type of paint to use. In comparison, acrylic gold looks a little lacklustre. However, varnishing over gold oil paint can be difficult and it is very important that you leave the paint to dry for at least an hour longer than you would normally. When you then apply the varnish, don't paint over it with too many brush strokes as the gold can wear off very easily and look tarnished.

ANTIQUING LIQUID

Sometimes also known as graining liquid, antiquing an object can be a very good way to finish it off. It gives a suitably aged look, very much in feel with my designs. Antiquing liquid is widely available and you simply paint it on as described by the manufacturer. Once it is dry, varnish over the top.

Alternatively, make your own antiquing liquid, which is something that I have done ever since starting to paint. Into an egg-cup full of varnish, add a tiny blob of raw umber oil paint (about the size of a drawing pin head) and mix together. Before applying the liquid, test it out on a similarly painted surface to check that the colour is right. Then, to apply the liquid, use either a soft cloth to wipe it all over the surface, or paint it onto the surface first and then wipe off with a soft cloth. This latter method is slightly better as it is easier to get the liquid into small corners with a paintbrush.

VARNISHES

A coat of varnish will give a tough finish to your painted object, ensuring that it will last for a long time and that any water-based paints don't smudge or smear, should some water land on it by mistake. Depending on what material the object is made of, various types of varnish are available. For wooden items where acrylic or emulsion paint has been used as a base coat, use an acrylic varnish. It is quick drying and is available in gloss or matt depending on the finish you are looking for. Otherwise, use a polyurethane varnish which gives a harder finish.

CHALK AND PENCIL

Chalk is particularly useful if you need to draw on an awkward and large surface, such as around the curve of a galvanized bucket. It is also preferable to use chalk rather than a pencil on an oil-based paint surface as it will show up better. However, for finer details, where you need a sharper image, use pencil.

STENCILLING MATERIALS

Preparing and using a stencil is gone into in greater detail on pages 14–15, but below is a list of the essential materials needed.

Stencilling materials (starting top left): repositionable spray glue, cut acetate, craft knife and protective cover, masking tape, marker pen, and roll of uncut acetate. These materials are resting on a cutting mat.

SHEET ACETATE OR OILED MANILLA BOARD

Either of these can be used to cut the stencil out from but I prefer to use acetate (and this is what is recommended throughout this book). Acetate is transparent, which makes it easier to check that the motif is correctly positioned, and the material is more malleable, making it good for covering lumps and bumps that might exist in the surface background.

MARKER PEN

It is best to use a fine nibbed marker pen so that you can transfer the motif very accurately.

CUTTING MAT

Professional cutting mats are available from art suppliers and shops, but they can be expensive so are really only worth buying if you are planning on doing a lot of stencilling. Alternatively, use a sheet of glass with masking tape wrapped around the edges to prevent any accidents, or a thick sheet of cardboard. If you are going to use the latter, make sure that it is quite smooth, with no previous cutting lines in it, as this could affect the way in which the craft knife cuts the new stencil.

MASKING TAPE

Masking tape is invaluable for stencilling as it can be re-used so easily. In addition to holding a stencil in place when cutting out, it can also be used to hold the stencil in place when it comes to painting over it, or it can act as an excellent mask for covering up parts of a design that you don't necessarily want to stencil through.

CRAFT KNIFE

These sharp knives really are the only blade to use when cutting out a stencil, although a small pair of sharp embroidery scissors can be used for fiddly work. For smooth, long, flowing lines, use the craft knife.

REPOSITIONABLE SPRAY GLUE

This sort of glue is wonderful for keeping a stencil in place when painting through it. Some people prefer to hold the stencil in place or to use masking tape instead, but for the best results, use repositionable spray glue. With this, the whole stencil will adhere well, leaving no possibility of paint running down behind the acetate, and this leaves the hands free for painting.

PREPARATION OF OBJECTS

WOOD

Particularly if the object is old, you will need to sand down any rough parts or edges before beginning to paint. The occasional lump or bump in the woodwork really doesn't matter for designs like mine as they add to the charm of the finished piece, so don't feel that you need to achieve the smoothest surface ever. After you have finished sanding, wipe over the object with a damp cloth and then leave it to dry thoroughly before beginning to paint.

particularly the case if the pots have been left in the garden for some time), there is really no preparation that needs to be done for these items.

METAL

For objects like the galvanised watering can and bread bin used in this book, you might need to remove any bits of rust using sandpaper or wire wool before beginning to paint. Also, these objects can frequently have sticky labels stuck on them. Use white spirit on a soft, clean cloth to remove any residue left over from attempting to peel off the labels. Wipe over the object with a damp cloth and leave it to dry thoroughly. You could also apply a coat of metal primer before beginning to paint.

TERRACOTTA

Apart from making sure that any terracotta plant pots that you are using are clean and dry (this is

PAINTING TECHNIQUES

APPLYING PAINT TO SURFACES

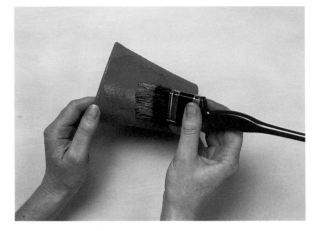

1 For the base coat of any object, never use more than a small amount of paint at a time. Dip your brush into the paint by no more than ½in (12mm) – never, on any account, push the brush in right up to the hilt.

2 The best way to remove any surplus paint is by pressing the bristles against the side of the tin, not the rim where paint may dry and lumps could fall into the paint later on. Then you should apply the paint in short, even brush strokes.

SHADING AND HIGHLIGHTING

Shading and highlighting is the essence of my painting style. These techniques are particularly important as they create a three-dimensional effect and suggest areas of light and reflection.

SHADING

1 Using black paint and a wet paintbrush or watered down paint, draw a line of paint along the underside of the motif, such as along the bottom of the goose's belly.

2 Using a finger or thumb, quickly blend in the line of paint, softening the colour into the body to give a gradual shaded effect.

HIGHLIGHTING

1 Apply white paint in exactly the same way as for shading, but slightly in from the edge of the motif to give an area of reflection.

2 Using a finger or thumb, quickly blend in the line to the required degree, as for shading.

STENCILS AND TEMPLATES

PREPARING A STENCIL

The materials needed for stencilling are listed on pages 10–11. Here I show you exactly how to make and use a stencil using the motifs given at the back of this book on pages 118–126.

1 Photocopy your chosen design. If you do not have access to a photocopier, trace the motif from the book. Position a piece of acetate over the design and trace it off using a marker pen. Use pieces of masking tape to keep the acetate steady.

2 Fasten the acetate down onto your cutting mat and use the craft knife to cut out the motif. To prevent accidents, pull the craft knife away from your body, not towards it. Try to move the knife in long, flowing lines to ensure a neat edge.

3 If you should make a mistake when cutting out the stencil, the acetate can easily be repaired with a small strip or two of sticky tape.

4 Spray the back of your stencil with repositionable glue, and position on your project. Using the stencil brush and paint, stencil the shape onto the surface.

SIZING A STENCIL

If you don't want to use the outlines in exactly the same size as they are reproduced at the end of this book they are easy to resize.

The easiest way is to use a photocopier with enlarging and reducing facilities – at the press of a button or two you will instantly see the outline copied to your specification. Alternatively, there is the good old-fashioned method of resizing by drawing squares over the existing outline. To enlarge the design, draw the same number of squares on a separate piece of paper, but much bigger. (The size depends on just how much you want to enlarge the design.) Then copy the design, transferring the lines exactly, square by square. To reduce the design, draw smaller squares.

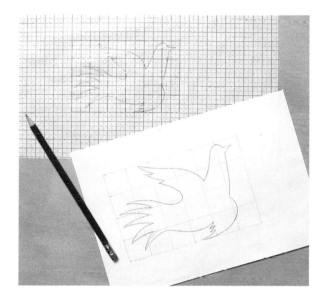

TEMPLATES

An alternative way of transferring the motif outline to your project is to make a card template. There are two ways of doing this. One is to trace the motif from the back of the book onto thin card using tracing paper, then cut around the outline using a craft knife or a pair of sharp scissors.

The other is to photocopy the motif from the back of the book and cut out the shape. Attach the paper shape to the card with small pieces of masking tape and draw around the outline. Cut out the motif shape from the card.

Size the motif up or down as for the stencil, either by using the photocopier or using squares. To use the template, spray the back of it with repositionable spray glue, position on your project and draw around the edge of the template using chalk

BASIC BORDERS

Borders of one kind or another are the final embellishment on a project and can be tailored to suit your taste. Several different borders and motifs are shown below and opposite together with simple instructions on how to paint them. Do remember to chalk in your border first·as this will make painting easier.

SIMPLE LEAF BORDER

A simple straight line with leaves radiating from it at regular intervals. Use mainly green paint but dip into yellow occasionally to add natural looking variation.

WAVY LEAF BORDER

The same principle as above, but make a gently undulating line first and then add your leaves.

FLOWER BORDER

Break up your leaf border with flowers. It is best to paint your flowers first and then join them together with leaves.

SUNFLOWER BORDER

For this versatile motif, use yellow paint to make a yellow disc with irregular edges and then add a raw umber centre. The leaves are slightly more delicate than the usual leaf borders.

EGG AND LEAF BORDER

This egg border looks appropriate with any of the fowl motifs. As the egg shape can be quite difficult to achieve freehand it is advisable to make a stencil. Simply stencil, paint, shade and highlight your eggs as described in any of the projects and then join together with undulating leaves.

LEMON BORDER

Follow exactly the same principle as with the egg and leaf border above. Again it would be useful to make a lemon stencil. Pears can also be used.

WHEAT BORDER

Follow the steps as shown above. It is advisable to use a little brown paint with your yellow to add some variation to the wheat colour.

ABSTRACT BORDERS

Here are three further, less fussy, borders. Use them to decorate edges and rims of drawers and boxes.

SPOTTED PIG

 The pig is an eternally popular farmyard animal. It also happens to be a very simple motif to paint, and the naive charm and rotund shape of this pig lend themselves perfectly to decorating an inexpensive round tin tray (as shown opposite). Pigs are also eminently suitable for buckets, sugar caddies and bread bins, and you can develop the simple outline into different colours and patterns. Overleaf you will find more ideas for pig designs which you can try.

In the project which follows, I chose an old fashioned 'muddy' mid-blue for the background colour. I avoided the predictable pink for the pig, choosing instead a creamy beige tone, which complements the antique blue. The finished item is both humorous and decorative, the simple leaf and flower pattern completing the colourful country theme.

The simple pig motif can be adapted to decorate a whole range of household items with charming and colourful designs. Shown here are a few ideas to try – a round wooden storage box, a biscuit tin, terracotta pots, a tin bucket, and even decorative wall plaques and hangers.

·PAINTING·THE·SPOTTED·PIG·TRAY·

·YOU·WILL·NEED·

PAINTS
Mid-sheen oil-based: mid-blue
Acrylic or emulsion: black, red, white, cream, raw umber, green

BRUSHES
1in (2.5cm) flat, Nos. 1, 4 and 6 artist's, stencil (optional)

OTHER ITEMS
Tin tray, white spirit, cloth, pig outline (see page 121), sheet acetate, marker pen, cutting mat, craft knife, masking tape or repositionable spray adhesive, chalk, small white saucer, paint tin or plate, antiquing fluid or polyurethane varnish

1 *Remove any labels with white spirit. Wash the tray in warm, soapy water to remove any grease or dust. Dry thoroughly. Using the 1in (2.5cm) flat brush, apply a coat of the oil-based paint to the tray's top surface and outer sides. To ensure an even painted surface, dip the brush head only ¼in (6mm) into the paint and apply in short, connecting strokes. When completely dry, add a second coat of base colour, once again taking care to produce an even background. Leave to dry.*

2 Following the instructions on pages 14–15,
  copy and cut out the pig stencil on page 121.
  Holding it firmly in place with masking tape,
paint over the stencil using the stencil brush and
black acrylic or emulsion paint. Allow the paint to
dry a little before lifting off the stencil. Alternatively,
use the stencil as a template and simply draw
around the inner edge using white chalk.

3 On a clean white
  saucer, make up
  the pig's body
colour by mixing a
little red with white or
cream, adding a tiny
amount of raw umber.
Once the stencil paint
has dried, begin to
paint the pig in more
detail, following the
step-by-step
instructions overleaf.
The body colour is
applied first, then the
details are built up on
top of this.

4 When you have completed the pig and it has
  fully dried, begin the border design. To get a
  fairly even circle around the pig on which to
paint the border of flowers and leaves, find an
object slightly smaller than your tray to draw
around – a paint tin or plate will be fine. Draw a
light chalk circle around the edge.

·PAINTING·YOUR·PIG·

1

Using the pig stencil, either draw or stencil the basic pig shape onto the prepared tray.

2

Fill in the pig shape with the body colour and using the No. 6 artist's brush, add the tail as shown. Add a second coat when dry, if required.

3

Using the No. 1 artist's brush, add fine black lines, nostrils, mouth and eye.

4

Using the No. 4 artist's brush, add spots. Vary their size and keep them quite uneven in shape.

5

Following the contours of the pig as shown, lightly shade with the No. 4 brush, using slightly watered-down black paint. Shade and highlight following the instructions and tips on pages 12–13. Apply the paint sparingly, gradually building up the shading to avoid a heavy layer of paint.

6

With the No. 1 artist's brush, lightly highlight ears, eye, back and tail in white.

7

Draw a circle in chalk around the pig. Lightly mark where the flowers are to be placed. Paint the flowers with the No. 4 artist's brush using the mixed dark pink paint, then join them with a fine line of green. Paint leaves in green with the No. 4 brush. (See also overleaf.)

5 *Mark lightly where you want your flowers to go. Think of the tray as a clock face and place the first flower at 12 o'clock, the second at 6 o'clock, then at 3 o'clock and 9 o'clock. Add in other flowers between these points as you feel necessary. Mix red with a small amount of white to create the petal colour. Paint the flowers using the No. 4 artist's brush, referring to page 16. Finally, fill in between the flowers with a leaf border, painted in green, using the No. 4 brush.*

6 *Paint the back of the tray using the base colour. Once this is dry, you can either varnish the tray or antique it and then varnish the painted surface (see page 10). Varnish is simply applied with a 1in (2.5cm) flat brush and left to dry in a dust-free environment. For an antiqued effect, use an antiquing or graining fluid (also see page 10). Varnish the tray once it has been antiqued. Your tray is ready for use a soon as the final coat of varnish is dry.*

ALTERNATIVE PIGS

There is always scope for personalising your projects by using a favourite breed or colour of pig. Here are a couple of alternative pigs to the one used on the tray. The great advantage of the black pig is that it doesn't need to be shaded, although a little highlighting, as you can see, enhances its shape. Its features need to be painted in a fine white. The eye needs to be done with particular care, or it will be completely lost. First highlight the eye area with white and then add the black eye. Similarly, the saddleback pig on the right is

also predominantly black, although its pink tummy will need shading.

The colours on the border can also be varied to those of your choice. You may like to try putting a bright border around the pig. Or, rather than using just one colour, use two alternately, say a russet brown and cream. Similarly, the leaves do not have to be done in green, they could be brown or grey. Try out different colour combinations on paper. Once you have found one you are happy with, use it on the tray.

A bucket painted with a saddleback pig motif. Use your pig stencil and adapt it, following the painting instructions above. Two shades of green have been used to create a vibrant background and border.

GOOSE WITH A TARTAN BOW TIE

This was one of the first items that I ever painted and despite my lack of confidence and skill, I found that the bucket was transformed by the background colour and its bold motif. The bucket's shape is also very effective for showing off cockerels and other farm animals. The goose, with his smart tartan bow tie, has always been my favourite – I particularly like the tartan pattern which is surprisingly easy to paint. All that you need to paint are a few lines crossing each other at right angles.

Painting the inside of your bucket is optional, but it is more versatile and functional with the inside unpainted as it can then be used for flowers, coal, water, or whatever else you care to put in it.

OVERLEAF The goose is such a popular and versatile motif and looks charming with or without a bow tie. Here you can see that I have varied the design by reversing it, changing the background colour of the bow, and – just for a change – painting polka dots in a contrasting colour in place of the tartan.

·PAINTING·THE·GOOSE·BUCKET·

·YOU·WILL·NEED·

PAINTS
Mid-sheen oil-based: red, gold
Acrylic or emulsion: white, yellow, green, black, red

BRUSHES
1½in (3.5cm) flat, Nos. 1, 4 and 6 artist's

OTHER ITEMS
Galvanised metal bucket (old or new will do), white spirit, soft cloth, glasspaper (optional), goose and tie outlines (see page 124), cutting mat, masking tape, craft knife, repositionable spray adhesive, chalk, high gloss polyurethane varnish

1 Make sure your bucket has a beautifully clean surface. First remove any labels with white spirit on a soft cloth and then dust down the bucket. If the bucket is an old one, you may also need to sand it down with medium grade glasspaper to remove any small lumps of rust. Finally, wash the bucket all over and then leave to dry thoroughly.

2 Using the 1½in (3.5cm) flat brush, apply a coat of the red oil-based paint. The galvanised surface takes the paint well, but it will need two coats, so leave it to dry overnight between coats. Take care when applying paint around the handles as drips and dribbles can occur. If you get any drips inside the bucket, wipe them off when the paint is wet using a soft rag and white spirit.

3 Following the instructions on pages 14–15, copy and cut out the goose template on page 124. Position it firmly in place using the repositionable spray glue, remembering to allow space for the goose's legs and feet at the bottom. Draw around the edge of the template with a piece of chalk and then paint the motif as detailed overleaf.

4 The goose's bow tie is a separate template and needs to be prepared as for Step 3. Position the template on the goose, draw around it with the chalk and then paint.

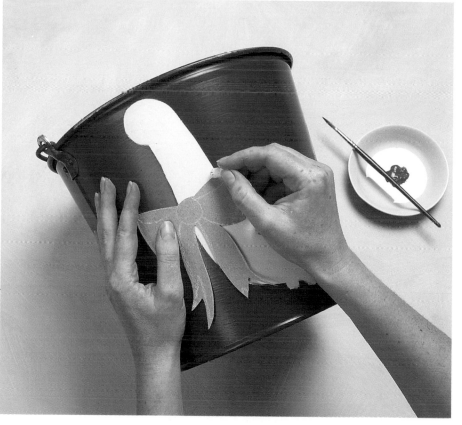

PAINTING·YOUR·GOOSE·

1

Fill the chalk outline using the white paint and No. 6 artist's brush. You will probably need two coats, so allow time for the first coat to dry.

2

For the beak, eyes and feet, carefully chalk on outlines. This gives you the opportunity to erase and try again, should you find it difficult to get the proportions right. When you are happy with the outlines, fill in with two coats of yellow paint using the No. 4 artist's brush.

3

Using the bow template, add a chalk outline of the bow at an appropriate part of the goose's neck as shown on the previous page. Fill in the outline with green paint.

4

When dry, paint in the details on the beak, eyes, wings, legs and feet in black using the No. 1 artist's brush.

5

To add the tartan lines to the bow, chalk in the grid as shown in diagram A below and then follow those lines with red acrylic or emulsion paint using the No. 1 artist's brush. When the red paint is dry, paint along the edge of the red in yellow paint, again using the No. 1 artist's brush. Shade and highlight following the instructions and tips on page 12–13.

Painting tartan on the bows

A

5. *For a finishing touch, use an oil-based gold paint on the rim, base and handle of the bucket. Alternatively, use a contrasting acrylic or emulsion colour such as green, which looks just as cheerful. Whichever colour you choose, paint it on with a No. 4 artist's brush using only small quantities of paint at a time to avoid any drips and runs.*

6. *Varnish the whole bucket with one coat of a high gloss polyurethane. Take particular care not to brush too much varnish over the gold paint as it can easily be tarnished in this way (see page 10 for guidance).*

ALTERNATIVE GEESE

There aren't too many ways of changing your goose in terms of colour, unless you are willing to embark upon a representation of some more exotic breed. To do this, search through books and magazines for a suitable picture and use this as your outline and basis from which to paint. You may well find that the picture you find needs to be resized, in which case use a photocopier, most of which are able to enlarge and reduce images very quickly and easily.

To add some variety to the design featured here, or to personalise your goose, you could start by using a different colour of paint for the bow tie. Or change the style of the bow by painting a different tartan or by using polka dots instead. Likewise, as pictured, give your bird a garland of flowers around his neck and add a floral border to your project (see pages 16–17). This will create a different impression entirely.

Here the goose template has been used to decorate a tray – the egg template from page 124 creates the ideal border for the design.

BLACK COCKEREL

These three mint-green tin containers are ideal for storing tea, coffee and sugar. If you wish, you can paint their contents in an appropriate place, on the lid for instance, or place an identifying sticker on the pots.

The handsome black cocks, with their red crests and faces, look at home in either a country kitchen or a more contemporary setting. The particular canisters I have used are inexpensive and, more importantly, are functional because the lid fits over a rim, rather than going over the side of the tin, where it would scratch the painted surface. It is well worth bearing this in mind when choosing your storage tins.

The leaf and flower border is optional, but it does sit well on the round tins. As an alternative to the black cockerel on a light background, paint a white cockerel on a dark background (see overleaf and page 47), shading and highlighting in reverse to that described on page 45. It looks particularly dramatic.

OVERLEAF By combining the cockerel with the egg, I have achieved all sorts of patterns here. Use eggs alone to make a border, as on the jug; paint them in pairs, as on the letter rack; or incorporate them into a leaf and flower border. Whatever you choose to do with the eggs, they will enliven the cockerel motif – it is, after all, why he exists.

·PAINTING·THE·COCKEREL· ·STORAGE·CONTAINERS·

· Y O U · W I L L · N E E D ·

PAINTS
Mid-sheen oil-based: pale green
Acrylic or emulsion: black, dark green, red, yellow, white, cream

BRUSHES
1½in (12mm) flat brush, Nos. 1, 4 and 6 artist's, stencil

OTHER ITEMS
Three tin storage containers, white spirit, clean cloth, cockerel and egg outlines (see pages 120 and 124), sheet acetate, marker pen, cutting mat, masking tape, craft knife, repositionable spray glue, pencil, chalk, polyurethane gloss varnish

1 *Make sure the containers are thoroughly clean before painting. If there are sticky labels on them, remove with white spirit on a clean cloth and then meticulously dust down the surface. Also remove the lids from the pots before beginning to paint.*

*2 Using the 1½in (3.5cm) flat brush, carefully
apply the first coat of the pale green oil-based
paint onto the pots and the lids and leave to
dry overnight. Apply the second coat of paint in the
same way.*

*3 Following the
instructions on
pages 14–15,
copy and cut out the
cockerel stencil on
page 120. Position it
firmly in place using
the repositionable
spray glue and then
paint over the stencil
using the stencil brush
and black acrylic or
emulsion paint. Leave
the paint to dry and
then continue to
decorate the cockerel
as described overleaf.*

*4 To add the egg on the lid, make a stencil from
the egg outline given on page 124 in the same
way as for the cockerel. Fix it in place as for
Step 3, then stencil and paint as described overleaf.*

·PAINTING·YOUR·COCKEREL·

1

Fill in the stencilled area with another coat of black paint, this time using the No. 6 artist's brush. Add a little flourish of dark green paint on the tail, neck and wing, also using the No. 6 artist's brush.

2

Using the red paint and No. 4 artist's brush, fill in the cockerel's crest and face.

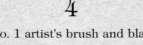

3

Add the beak, eye and legs in yellow paint, also using the No. 4 artist's brush. Remember that you can pencil or chalk these in first in order to get the proportions right. Add a second coat of yellow paint when the first has dried.

4

Using the No. 1 artist's brush and black paint, fill in the details on the eye, beak, crest and legs.

5

Using the No. 1 artist's brush and slightly watered-down white paint, add the white cheek and also the detail of eye, neck, wing, leg and tail feathers.

6

Shading your cockerel is fairly limited on the black area, but it can be done on the cockerel's face and legs, as shown here.

7

Highlighting with white also makes an impact (follow the instructions and tips on pages 12–13). Pay particular attention to the tail, wing and neck.

8

The stencilled egg in the centre of the lid is stencilled with a cream acrylic or emulsion paint and then shaded around the edges to give it some depth. A white highlight will also give the impression of a sheen on the egg. Add the final touch of a border of flowers and leaves, as described overleaf.

5 Once the
cockerels are
finished, add any
borders that you feel
are appropriate. For
the flowers, I have
mixed white with a
little red. Place them at
fairly regular intervals
around the top and
base of the pot,
remembering that the
closer together you
paint the flowers, the
easier it will be to join
them with an even
border of leaves.

6 Using the No. 1
artist's brush,
join each flower
to the next one with a
thin green line. Add
the leaves with the No.
6 artist's brush, as
described on page 16.
Once all the paint has
thoroughly dried, cover
the storage containers
and their lids with a
single coat of
polyurethane gloss
varnish.

ALTERNATIVE COCKERELS

I have three styles of cockerel that I use regularly. The black one (as shown in the project), a white one and a handsome coloured one. For the white cockerel, follow the instructions given for the black bird on pages 43–6, but substituting white for black.

To paint the coloured cockerel, use a dark green for the main body and highlight the tail with a little yellow. When dry, paint the wing in a rust colour and then the neck and head in a yellow, perhaps streaking the yellow with a little rust for depth. When the paint is dry, add the crest, beak, eyes and legs following steps 2–7 on pages 44–45, as before. Continue to follow the instructions and you will have a beautiful coloured rooster.

Although these two cockerels have been painted to look different, their outlines have been taken from the same stencil. To reverse a stencil, clean it thoroughly and then simply flip it over.

SHAGGY SHEEP

Shaker boxes are widely available these days in either an oval or round shape. Unadorned, they are both attractive and useful, but they are a real pleasure to paint and make a very special gift either empty or when filled with appropriate goodies. Look out for the cheaper, plywood Shaker boxes as they have a nice finish onto which you can apply your paint.

I have chosen two slightly different shades of green for the boxes and also painted a lovely contrasting colour on their insides. My sheep are very basic and simple and would not bear close scrutiny by a shepherd, but they are effective and, with the floral border, look very much at home on these boxes. If you are feeling in the mood for further embellishment, a small motif on the inside of the lid (either a sheep or flower) makes a nice surprise detail when the box is opened.

OVERLEAF   Of course, you needn't feel obliged to paint just one motif on an item. On this old blanket box I chose to paint several different animals, each of which is featured in this book. The pig is on pages 18–27 and the cow on pages 68–77. Notice, too, how I altered the sheep running around the bottom rim of the bucket – by painting their legs at different angles you can easily achieve quite a different personality for your animals.

·PAINTING·THE·SHEEP·SHAKER·BOX·

·YOU·WILL·NEED·

PAINTS
Acrylic or emulsion: black, brown, white, red, yellow, green

BRUSHES
1½in (3.5cm) flat, Nos. 1, 4 and 6 artist's, stencil

OTHER ITEMS
Shaker-style boxes made of wood (two, if possible), sheep outline (see pages 122–3), sheet acetate, marker pen, cutting mat, masking tape, craft knife, repositionable spray glue, glasspaper (fine grade), satin acrylic varnish or antiquing liquid

1. *Paint the base colour of your choice (here, a lovely grassy green) onto the box. Use good, even strokes as only one coat of paint should be needed and it will dry within 30 minutes. Paint the base and lid separately as they will be easier to decorate in this way.*

2 *Paint the inside of the box and lid using either the same colour as the outside or a contrast. Leave to dry.*

3 *Following the instructions on pages 14–15, copy and cut out a sheep stencil from pages 122–3. Position it firmly in place using the repositionable spray glue and then paint over the stencil using the stencil brush and black paint. Take care with the spacing of the figures around the edges; the more evenly spaced they are, the better. Leave the paint to dry and then continue to decorate the sheep as described overleaf.*

·PAINTING·YOUR·SHEEP·

1

When you have stencilled your sheep onto the lid and around the base, use the stencil brush dipped into brown, black and white paints to paint the bodies. With a rhythmical stabbing action, you can create a wonderful woolly effect. Keep building up the colours until you feel the sheep's wool looks correct.

2

If you want to change the breed of sheep for your box, wait until the paint has dried, then paint over the head and legs with white paint and the No. 4 brush.

3

Paint in the sheep's ears, eyes and mouth, and the few lines representing the joints and feet. Use the No. 1 artist's brush for this.

4

Shade and highlight the sheep following the instructions and tips on pages 12–13. Don't forget to add the sparkle in the sheep's eye.

5

For the border of flowers on the lid, mark a guideline as described in step 4 overleaf. Then paint the border as described in step 5 on page 26.

6

Join the flowers together with a thin green line using the No. 1 artist's brush.

7

Add leaves using the No. 4 artist's brush as described on page 16.

8

Around the edge of the lid, add further flowers.

9

Join them together with a thin line.

10

Add the leaves along the line that you have just painted.

ALTERNATIVE BORDER

Paint the sides of the lid in white using the No. 6 brush.

In pencil, add zigzag lines.

Fill with black paint.

BORDER AROUND THE BASE

To make a border around the base of your box, first add flowers at regular intervals, then join with a thin green line, as before. Finally, add the leaves.

4 When you have completed the sheep and they
have dried fully, begin the border design. To
get an even circle around the sheep on which
to paint the border of flowers and leaves, find an
object slightly smaller than your box lid to draw
around – a paint tin or plate will be fine. Draw a
light chalk circle around the edge.

5 When you are
happy with the
sheep and
borders, and the paint
has completely dried,
use the fine grade
glasspaper to gently
sand the edges of the
box. This will antique
them slightly.

6 Use the finish of
your choice, such
as a quick drying
satin acrylic varnish or
an antiquing liquid
lightly rubbed onto the
surface (or painted on
and rubbed off, see
page 10) to create a
sheen and protective
coating for your box.

ALTERNATIVE SHEEP

On this particular project I have varied the painting possibilities of the sheep by showing it with a black face, a white face, and in a running or static position (see pages 48–51). Another possibility to vary the look of either the white- or black-faced sheep is to add horns to turn it into a handsome ram. It will probably be best to pencil or chalk your horn shapes in first and then mix a little yellow and brown to paint over your sketch.

I have also shown an illustration here of a sheep with a lamb at its side. The lamb is quite simple to do and adds a very nice touch to the composition. Prepare a stencil using the large motif given on page 122, and stencil the outline in place before painting the fully grown sheep, otherwise you will end up with a very textured piece of painting. When painting your lamb, note that it is not quite as woolly as the fully grown adult sheep.

LEMONS AND PEARS

Painting unglazed terracotta is a very rewarding task. Even without any embellishment, the porous surface takes water-based paints very well and they dry quickly so that work isn't held up by waiting for paint to dry.

Onto these dramatic black pots I have stencilled and painted both pears and lemons in a strongly contrasting yellow. The shading and highlighting of such fruit is very important to give them depth and that beautiful patina that so often appears, particularly on ripe pears.

Here, I have added a leaf border around the top of the pots and also pairs of leaves on each piece of fruit. Of course, not all picked lemons and pears have leaves remaining so you might decide to paint the fruits without their leaves, or perhaps paint a mixture – some with, others without. Whichever you choose, terracotta pots like these look stunning either on a conservatory window sill or in a garden.

OVERLEAF As a slightly more sophisticated motif, the lemons and pears lend themselves to a variety of items and background colours. Here, they look equally good on green, Mediterranean blue, white and dark blue. They also make useful border motifs and combine particularly well with the Dove of Peace and Topiary Trees projects included in this book (see pages 78–87 and 98–107).

·PAINTING·THE·LEMON·AND·PEAR· ·TERRACOTTA·POTS·

· Y O U · W I L L · N E E D ·

PAINTS
Oil-based: gold (optional)
Acrylic or emulsion: black, yellow, white, green, brown (or raw umber and gold)

BRUSHES
1½in (3.5cm) flat, Nos. 4 and 6 artist's, stencil

OTHER ITEMS
Two terracotta pots, white spirit, soft cloth, lemon and pear outlines (see page 123), sheet of acetate, marker pen, cutting mat, masking tape, craft knife, repositionable spray glue, chalk, varnish or antiquing liquid

1 Carefully dust down the pots and remove any sticky labels (surplus stickiness can be removed using a little white spirit on a soft cloth). Then apply the base coat of black acrylic or emulsion paint using the 1½in (3.5cm) flat paintbrush. Only one coat will be needed. Remember to use good, even brush strokes as outlined on page 13.

2 Following the instructions on pages 14–15, copy and cut out the lemon and pear stencils on page 123. When the base coat is dry (which is relatively quick, depending on the weather), apply the stencils, positioning them firmly in place using the repositionable spray glue. Then paint over the stencils using the stencil brush and yellow acrylic or emulsion paint.

3 Take care to apply the fruits at fairly even intervals and it also helps to place the stencils at random angles. The fruits then look more realistic. Leave the paint to dry and then continue to decorate the lemons and pears with shading and highlighting as described overleaf.

·PAINTING·YOUR·LEMONS·AND·PEARS·

1

When the stencilled
base coat is dry, the stencils
will be a pale yellow.

2

To enhance the colouring,
fill the stencilled shapes
with a further coat of
yellow paint, but this time
using the No. 6 artist's
brush. Follow the natural
contours of the fruit with
your brush strokes.

3

Shade and highlight the
fruit following the
instructions and tips on
pages 12–13. Remember
that it is better to build up
the shading gradually than
to apply it too heavily in
the first place.

4

Add stalks and speckles with a dark brown or raw umber using the No. 4 artist's brush.

5

Using green paint with a touch of yellow and a No. 4 artist's brush, paint in the leaves. The technique for leaf painting is covered more thoroughly on page 16.

6

Prepare the leaf border as described in Step 4 overleaf. Then paint over the chalk line with green paint and the No. 1 artist's brush and add leaves as above, again using the No. 4 artist's brush.

4. For the wavy leaf border on this pot, draw a line in chalk around the rim before painting over it. Also add leaves to each lemon with chalk. The advantage of roughing something out in chalk first is that if you go wrong it is easy to rub out and draw again.

5. Once you are happy with your leaves and border outline, paint in the leaf border as described on the previous page.

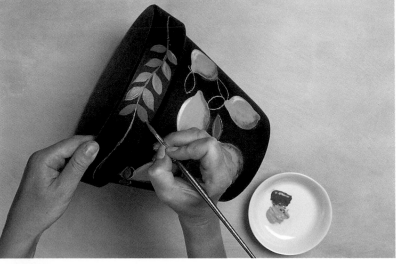

6. As an optional extra, adding gold as a border or onto the rim does look very dramatic in contrast to the black. Allow extra drying time before varnishing if you have added gold because the gold can easily become slightly tarnished-looking when applying varnish.

ALTERNATIVE LEMONS AND PEARS

Although there aren't too many ways that you can vary the actual look of the lemon and pear motifs, there is always the potential for altering the overall appearance by variations in background colour and where you place the motifs. On the main project in this chapter they are placed at random on the terracotta pots, but with a little planning it is possible to paint the fruits in rows, even alternating them. To do this, you will need to divide the project into bands (use chalk or pencil), stencil your first fruit in place and then use your stencil as a guide to see how many you can fit onto the project. As you can see, I have joined together the lemons and pears with leaves.

COW AND
WHEATSHEAF

 The best thing about bread bins is that you don't have to use them to store bread. I have one for pasta, one for flour and one for dog biscuits. Furthermore, there are many old enamel bread bins to be found and this is the perfect project for one that is in need of a face lift.

Although I have a weakness for the more traditional black and white or brown and white cows, I thought that this chocolate brown cow on the antiqued creamy background made a slightly more subtle combination. Once you have your cow stencil though, you can paint whichever breed of cow most appeals to you.

The wheatsheaves on the lid and on the bin itself are simple to paint and add some welcome lightness to this design. Because the cow's body is so long, it is all too easy for this design to become a little dense, so if you decide to paint a similarly coloured animal, ensure you paint it onto a pale coloured background.

OVERLEAF Varying the look of your cows is most straightforward. Outline areas of colour on the background using a piece of chalk or a pencil and once you are happy with the shapes, simply fill them in using a No. 4 artist's paintbrush. For particularly fine spots, use a No. 1 brush.

·PAINTING·THE·COW·BREAD·BIN·

·YOU·WILL·NEED·

PAINTS
Mid-sheen oil-based: magnolia, gold (optional)
Acrylic or emulsion: black, brown, white, red, yellow, green

BRUSHES
1½in (3.5cm) flat, Nos. 1, 4 and 6 artist's, stencil

OTHER ITEMS
Enamel bread bin (old or new), white spirit, soft cloth, glasspaper (optional), cow outline (see page 119), sheet acetate, marker pen, cutting mat, masking tape, craft knife, repositionable spray adhesive, antiquing liquid, polyurethane gloss varnish

1 Make sure your bread bin has a beautifully clean surface. Remove any labels with white spirit on a soft cloth and then carefully dust it down. If the bread bin is an old one, you may also need to sand it down with medium grade glasspaper to remove any small lumps of rust. Following all this preparation, wash the bread bin and then leave it to dry thoroughly.

2 Apply the first coat of the magnolia oil-based paint using the 1½in (3.5cm) flat brush. Paint it on carefully and sparingly to avoid drips and runs, especially around the handles. Leave the paint to dry thoroughly and then apply a second coat of paint.

3 Following the instructions on pages 14–15, copy and cut out the cow stencil on page 119. Position it firmly in place using the repositionable spray glue and then paint over the stencil using the stencil brush and black acrylic or emulsion paint. Continue to paint the rest of the cow as described overleaf.

·PAINTING·YOUR·COW·

1

Mix brown paint with a little white to make a soft brown colour. Carefully paint onto the stencilled area using the No. 6 artist's brush for the body, but change to a smaller No. 4 for the legs, tail and heads.

2

Mix some antique pink (white with very small amounts of red and brown) and paint the cow's muzzle and udder using the No. 4 artist's brush.

3

Using the No. 1 artist's brush and black paint, add detail lines as shown. Use the dark brown paint and No. 4 artist's brush for the cow's hooves.

4

If you wish to add horns to the cow, use a mixture of brown and yellow paints. Chalk them in place first as a guideline for your paintbrush. You may find that the horns require two coats.

5

Your cow should now be ready for shading. Pay particular attention around the udder, chin and legs.

6

Carefully highlight appropriate parts of your cow with a little watered down white paint.

7

To create the grassy effect under the cow's feet, use the stencil brush to stipple on green paint with some yellow highlights. To create this effect, put a very small amount of both colours on the brush and use sharp stabbing movements.

TO PAINT THE WHEAT MOTIF

Lightly pencil the wheat motif in the size you require for your project, copying the image illustrated. Use a No. 1 brush for the stalks and spindles and a No. 4 brush for the ears and leaves. Use a tiny amount of brown with the yellow as this adds depth to the colour and image.

4 After you have finished painting the cow, add the wheat motif where required. In this case, I have positioned it on the lid. Paint the motif as described on the previous page.

5 Decorate the bread bin handles with either the gold oil-based paint or a contrasting acrylic or emulsion colour. The rim of the lid and handle on the lid should also be painted to match.

6 I have also added an extra inner border of acrylic red around the rim of the lid. Painted on with a No. 4 artist's brush, this is a useful way of disguising any wobbly or ragged edges of the trim colour. Antique the surface quite heavily with antiquing liquid before applying a polyurethane gloss varnish. (If you used gold paint, see page 10 for information about varnishing over gold.)

ALTERNATIVE COWS

One of the easiest ways of varying your cow outline is to turn it into a sleeping cow. The cow to the right on the box lid shows just such a resting cow whose outline should be quite easy to copy and position on your bread bin, or whatever object you are decorating.

Once you have your basic cow outline, whether it is the one featured on the previous pages or the one to the right, it is quite simple to draw in patches onto a white background and create your own black and white, brown and white, beige and white or even terracotta and white cow.

To do this effectively, it is best to paint one or two coats of white onto your stencilled shape and then pencil in the appropriate places for your patches to go. By pencilling them in you can easily amend the patches should you find they are too big, too small, or in the wrong place. Paint the patches and finish off by filling in the muzzle and udder in pink, and adding horns.

This hat box has been decorated with cows charging around their field and a rather somnambulant beast. Such variations are fun to create, giving originality to your designs.

DOVE OF PEACE

Of the ten projects shown in this book, I think that this is my favourite. The dove motif is one of the simplest to do and combines beautifully with flowers and leaves, as you can see on the pot standing on top of the drawer unit. On the unit itself, I have used just simple line and dot borders on the drawers and surrounding base, but if you prefer a more floral effect, flowers painted at the corner of each drawer joined together by a leaf border look very pretty around the dove. For details on painting this border and some other ideas see pages 16–17.

The drawers that I used came in a basic white wood which meant that I was able to paint directly onto them with water-based emulsion. I chose a warm rusty red which contrasts well with the white birds and the green trim. For a variation in colour, I painted the insides of the drawers in the same green as the trim.

OVERLEAF   The beauty of stencil designs is that they can be enlarged or reduced very easily (see page 15) to suit your requirements. The blue card with green border on the left uses the dove in two different sizes, and the wooden box at the top uses three sizes. The dove also combines very well with other designs in this book, most particularly the pears that appear on pages 58–67.

·PAINTING·THE·DOVE·CHEST·OF·DRAWERS·

1 Remove all the drawers and prepare them and their surround by sanding down any rough edges with medium grade glasspaper and then dust down with a damp cloth. If there is some sticky residue left from any labels that were on the drawers, remove it with white spirit on a cloth.

2 Paint the fronts, sides and
upper edges of each drawer
and the shell with the
acrylic or emulsion base coat. I
used different colours for the
drawers and the shell, but you
may decide to use the same
colour for both. Use short, even
strokes and in this way you
should only need one coat of
base colour.

3 Following the instructions
on pages 14–15, copy and
cut out one of the dove
stencils on page 126. Position it
firmly in place using the
repositionable spray glue and
then paint over the stencil using
the stencil brush and white
acrylic or emulsion paint.

4 To reverse the dove design,
cut out and use the other
dove stencil from page 126.
Alternatively, wipe over the side
of the stencil that you have been
using to remove any residue of
paint and then flip over the
stencil and use as before.
Continue to paint the doves as
described overleaf.

·PAINTING·YOUR·DOVE·

1
The dove outline after it has
been stencilled with white paint.

2
Add the beak and eyes using
the No. 4 artist's brush and
yellow paint.

3
Using the No. 1 artist's brush
and black paint, carefully paint
in the details on the beak, eye,
wings and tail. If you prefer, you
can pencil this in first.

4
Shade the dove following the
instructions and tips on pages
12–13. Try to do this as
delicately as possible because
the black contrasts so strongly
with the white.

5

With a ruler and pencil, draw lines around the edge of each drawer. Use a measurement of approximately ½in (12mm) from the edge of the drawers.

6

When you have drawn all the lines, paint over them with green paint using the No. 4 artist's brush.

7

Add coloured dots within the border made by the drawer's edge and the lines you have just painted. Dots can be surprisingly difficult to paint, so practise first on a piece of scrap paper.

8

As an optional extra, add leaves to the doves that appear on the top and sides of the chest of drawers. Pencil in the stem first, paint over the top in green and then paint the leaves (see page 16).

5 For some
decorative
details, paint a
fine line ½in (12mm)
in from the edge all
around the drawer
fronts. Finish with
small dots painted in a
contrasting colour.

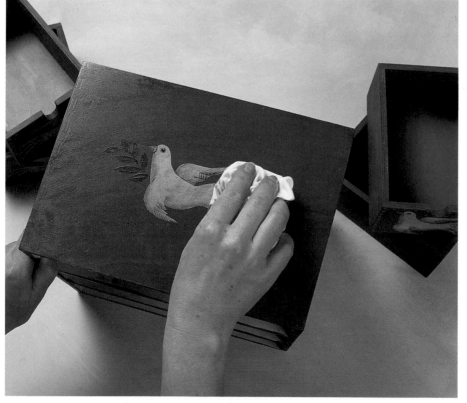

6 To finish and seal
the chest of
drawers, brush
on antiquing liquid
and then wipe off most
of the surplus with a
soft cloth (see page
10). Don't forget to
repeat this on the sides
of the drawers, too.

ALTERNATIVE DOVES

There aren't too many ways that you can change the look of your flying dove. However, the way that you border the dove project can make a great difference to the overall finish. In the project illustrated on the previous pages I have tried not to let the design become fussy or floral. However, by adding lots of flowers and leaves, you can make a very pretty project. Alternatively, add some fruit such as lemons and pears (see pages 63–66 for painting instructions), to the border as these fruits can look very attractive with your lovely dove.

Doves are just as happy standing still as soaring through the air. Use the dove to the right as an outline for a template and paint it on a jar just like the one shown below.

Alternatively use the soaring dove from the project to decorate your jar, or create the design illustrated on page 4 by painting a garland around the dove. This would be ideal for decorating a round tray or lid.

AURICULA

Over the past few years, the auricula, a member of the Primula family, has become increasingly popular and can be found decorating many a household item, including wallpapers and fabrics. Auriculas are unusual plants and quite difficult to grow successfully in their pure form. Perhaps this elusive charm is what makes the painted items so sought after. The flowers come in a variety of wonderful deep colours and my own interpretation rather simplifies the richness and beauty of the plant. Combined with the blue and white pot, however, the effect is not too bad and you have the scope to choose your background to complement your favourite coloured flower.

I like these Victorian-looking enamel jugs and feel that they are suitably elegant in shape to carry this particular auricula design. When finished, your jug can be used for flowers, but treat it with care as jugs are always rather vulnerable to knocks when used for pouring.

OVERLEAF   For variety, the flower heads can be different colours, of course, and you can have great fun developing all sorts of patterns to decorate the pots, too. Notice the small pots above the cupboard to the left of the picture: they just feature the auricula flower heads and some leaves, making a charmingly simple addition.

·PAINTING·THE·AURICULA·ENAMEL·JUG·

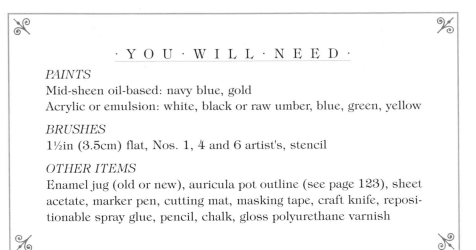

· Y O U · W I L L · N E E D ·

PAINTS
Mid-sheen oil-based: navy blue, gold
Acrylic or emulsion: white, black or raw umber, blue, green, yellow

BRUSHES
1½in (3.5cm) flat, Nos. 1, 4 and 6 artist's, stencil

OTHER ITEMS
Enamel jug (old or new), auricula pot outline (see page 123), sheet acetate, marker pen, cutting mat, masking tape, craft knife, repositionable spray glue, pencil, chalk, gloss polyurethane varnish

1 *On an enamel jug like this one there is no preparation that needs to be done, but do make sure it is clean and dry before painting. Then paint the navy blue oil-based paint onto the jug using the 1½in (3.5cm) brush. Try to paint the handle as well, as this will make the gold paint much easier to apply at the end.*

2 *To finish off the jug neatly, turn it upside down and paint the base, using the same oil-based paint. The jug can be left upside down to dry. For a neat finish, the jug will need two coats of paint. But before applying the second coat, allow the first to dry overnight.*

*3 Following the
instructions on
pages 14–15,
copy and cut out the
auricula pot stencil
on page 123. Position
it firmly in place
towards the bottom of
the jug using the
repositionable spray
glue and then paint
over the stencil using
the stencil brush and
white acrylic or
emulsion paint.*

*4 When the paint
has dried, remove
the stencil and
apply a further coat of
the white acrylic or
emulsion paint over the
pot. Then decorate the
jug as described
overleaf.*

·PAINTING·YOUR·AURICULA·

1

The auricula plant pot painted white with
two coats of acrylic or emulsion paint.

2

When the white paint is dry, sketch in an
ellipse and fill with either the black or raw
umber paint to represent soil. Use the No. 4
artist's brush.

3

When the paint is dry, decorate the pot with
the blue paint. First sketch the design lightly
onto the pot with a pencil and then paint
over the lines using the No. 4 artist's brush
and slightly watered-down blue paint (this
makes a marginally less opaque finish). Add
blue dots around the rim and base.

4

When you have finished painting the blue
pattern onto the white pot and it has dried,
shade along the sides and top and base.
Shade following the instructions and tips
that are given on page 12.

5

Find the centre of the pot and from there,
draw a slightly curving stalk approximately
2½in (6cm) high. Once it is drawn to your
satisfaction, paint it in using the green paint,
slightly lightened with white, and the No. 4
artist's brush.

6

For the auricula head, study my picture and
then arrange a group of flower heads around
the top of the stalk. Sketch them in first
with chalk. When you are happy with the
proportions, paint them in using the yellow
paint on the No. 4 artist's brush.

7

Using the No. 1 artist's brush, carefully paint around the edge of each flower head in white, outlining the edge of each petal as shown.

8

Again using the No. 4 artist's brush, fill the centre of each flower with white.

9

When the white paint is dry, fill with yellow as shown. It should look a little like a poached egg.

10

Finally, at the centre of your 'egg', place a tiny white dot.

11

Pencil or chalk in your leaves so that the larger ones reach out beyond the pot and the smaller ones creep over the front edge. Paint them in using the green paint and either the No. 4 or No. 6 brush.

12

Outline the leaves in white using the No. 1 artist's brush.

13

To add some depth to the leaves, shade a little at the base of the leaves and stalk, as described on page 12.

14

Highlight the leaves quite heavily (as described on page 14) to represent the characteristic whiteness that appears on auricula leaves.

5. On some of the other projects in this book I have suggested that a gold trim for the handles and rims is optional. But for this auricula, I really do recommend the addition of some gold, as it enhances the formality, and hence attractiveness, of the composition.

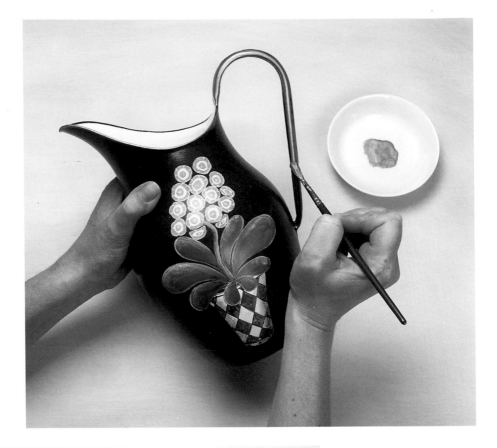

6. Paint on a coat of rich gloss polyurethane varnish to bring out the beautiful colours of your handsome jug. See page 10 for advice on painting over gold oil-based paint which can all too easily become sullied.

ALTERNATIVE AURICULAS

The most obvious way of changing or varying your auricula design is to use a different colour for the flower. Study botanical pictures and photographs and then interpret them in a simplified form onto your painting. A deep red colour looks beautiful and instead of edging the petals with a fine white line use pink so that the edging doesn't contrast too sharply with the deep colour of the petal.

Another permutation is to put your plant in a plain terracotta pot instead of the blue and white pot featured on the previous pages. You can always add some interest to your terracotta by ageing it. Add some hairline 'cracks' with a No. 1 brush and some raw umber paint and then before shading and highlighting, put a little watered down green paint on your fingertip and dab onto the terracotta to create a moss or lichen effect.

Paint your auricula flowerheads in any shade and add as many or as few leaves as you like. Change the length of stem, too: there is no need to be shy of adapting these designs.

TOPIARY TREES

There is a classic timelessness to this simple topiary motif that makes it fit in with many themes and environments. When I was planning this particular design, I felt that the watering can would make an extremely good background for it because of its horticultural use. I also found that the taller shape accommodates the trees perfectly. As with the Goose With A Tartan Bow Tie (see pages 28–37), a template of the tree may be easier to use than a stencil. The ridges commonly found in galvanised ware can make stencilling quite tricky and it is easier to keep a template steady. Once you have drawn on the motif's outline it just remains necessary to fill it in.

Some highlighting and shading on the trees and pots is particularly essential to prevent them from looking too flat. The small amount of white highlighting gives the pots and their trees an authentic sheen as if they were standing in the garden on a sunny day.

OVERLEAF   With its obvious garden theme, the topiary design lends itself to items for the garden or conservatory such as terracotta pots, watering cans, tin trays, and containers for all those small but essential pieces of gardening equipment. On some of these items I have chosen to decorate the topiary tree containers with blue and white patterns for a spot of variety.

·PAINTING·THE·TOPIARY·WATERING·CAN·

· Y O U · W I L L · N E E D ·

PAINTS
Mid-sheen oil-based: wheat, gold
Acrylic or emulsion: rust, green, yellow, raw umber/brown, black, white

BRUSHES
1½in (3.5cm) flat, Nos. 4 and 6 artist's, stencil

OTHER ITEMS
Galvanised metal watering can (old or new), white spirit, soft cloth, glasspaper (medium grade) (optional), topiary outlines (see page 118), cutting mat, masking tape, craft knife, repositionable spray glue, antiquing fluid, polyurethane gloss varnish

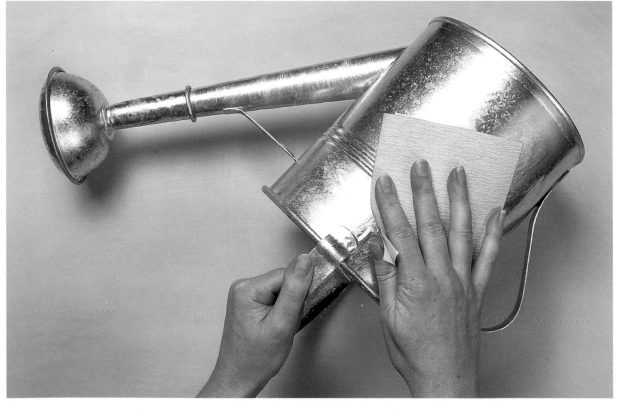

1 *Make sure your watering can has a meticulously clean surface. First remove any labels with white spirit on a soft cloth and then dust down. If the watering can is an old one,*

you may also need to sand it down with medium grade glasspaper to remove any small lumps of rust. Finally, wash the watering can and then leave it to dry thoroughly.

2 Paint on the first coat of
the wheat oil-based paint.
There will be some
awkward little spots on the
watering can so take care,
particularly under the handles
and around the spout and rose.
Watch out for drips and dribbles,
although this problem should
not occur if you use only a small
amount of paint on the brush.
Apply two coats of the base
colour, leaving the watering can
to dry overnight before painting
the second coat.

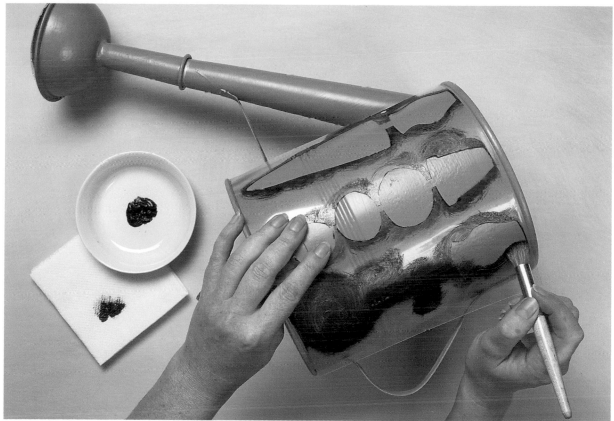

3 Following the instructions on pages 14–15,
copy and cut out the topiary stencil on page
118. Position it firmly in place using the
repositionable spray glue and then paint over the
stencil using the stencil brush and black acrylic or
emulsion paint. Then paint the motifs as described
in detail overleaf.

·PAINTING·YOUR·TOPIARY·

1

Begin by filling in the terracotta pots using the rust acrylic or emulsion and the No. 4 artist's brush. The pots may require two coats of paint, in which case leave sufficient time for the first coat to dry before applying the second.

2

Using either the stencil brush or No. 6 artist's brush, paint in the foliage. Use a short stabbing motion with the brush to create an uneven edge and texture. Dip the brush into green and yellow paint alternately to create variation of tone and depth in the painting.

3

Using the raw umber or brown paint and No. 4 artist's brush, fill in the tree trunks and paint an ellipse of soil in the terracotta pots to create a three-dimensional effect.

4

Shade and highlight the pots and topiary trees as illustrated. This will greatly enhance their depth. For instructions and tips on shading and highlighting, see pages 12–13.

5

To add even more interest to your trees, you can add lemons and pears as shown in the project on pages 58–67.

4 To decorate the top of the watering can, paint a thin green line and add leaves as described on page 16.

5 Carefully paint the watering can edges with the gold oil-based paint. If gold is not available, use either green or rust; either will combine well with the design. Two coats will usually be required.

6 When completely dry, antique and then varnish the watering can. If you used gold paint, see the advice on page 10 for varnishing over gold as it can all too easily become sullied.

ALTERNATIVE TOPIARY

I love the simplicity of the topiary motif but there are some quite straightforward ways to make it a little more elaborate. First, instead of the plain terracotta pots, you could create blue and white pots following the instructions for the pot in the auricula project (see pages 88–97). In addition to this, adding lemons, pears or apples to your trees will add some colour and create a completely different look. Sketch in your fruits first, and then paint in the colour required. When the paint is dry, shade and highlight the fruit.

CHINA TEAPOT

 Finally, this teapot motif moves away from the farmyard and floral images and is versatile as you can choose colours and designs on your teapot to suit your kitchen. Once you have your basic teapot shape, you can invent or copy all sorts of patterns and motifs to adorn it. I chose this particular design of biscuit tin because the lid can be frequently removed and replaced without damaging the paintwork which makes it suitable for everyday use.

For this particular project, I chose a smart blue and white teapot on a cheerful yellow background. The heart shapes can either be stencilled on or drawn in pencil and then painted using a No. 4 artist's brush, unless the design is very detailed, in which case use a No. 1 artist's brush. For added detail, I also painted around the narrow rim of the lid with the same background colour as used on the teapot and finished it off with some fine blue dots. The handle of the lid has been highlighted, too, with the same colours, but this time I painted on just a simple blue line to prevent the whole design from becoming overly fussy.

OVERLEAF   There are several variations in shape for the teapots featured in this picture. Round and square, spouts with 'V's at the pouring end and plain, elliptical finishes, lids that sit on top or fit snugly into the pot itself. Adapt the design given here, or go ahead and create your own, unique teapot.

·PAINTING·THE·TEAPOT·BISCUIT·TIN·

·

·YOU·WILL·NEED·

PAINTS
Mid-sheen oil-based: yellow
Acrylic or emulsion: white, black, blue

BRUSHES
1½in (3.5cm) flat, Nos. 1, 4 and 6 artist's, stencil

OTHER ITEMS
Metal biscuit tin (old or new with a lid that fits inside rather than
outside), white spirit, clean cloth, teapot outline (see page 125),
sheet acetate, marker pen, cutting mat, masking tape, craft knife,
repositionable spray adhesive, pencil, antiquing liquid,
polyurethane varnish (satin or gloss)

1 *Before beginning to paint the biscuit tin, make
sure it is meticulously clean and dust free. If
there is residue from a sticky label or two,
gently remove this with some white spirit on an old
but clean piece of cloth.*

2 *Remove the lid from the biscuit tin and paint
on the first coat of the oil-based paint on the
outside only – do not paint inside the lid. The
tin will need two coats of paint, so leave it to dry
overnight before applying the second coat.*

3 Following the
instructions on
pages 14–15,
copy and cut out the
teapot stencil on page
125. Position it firmly
in place using the
repositionable spray
glue. Then paint over
the stencil using the
stencil brush and
white acrylic or
emulsion paint.
Continue to paint the
rest of the teapot as
described overleaf.

4 To decorate the
biscuit tin lid,
paint the knob
and trim in a
contrasting colour.
Hearts can be
stencilled around the
top of the lid, as
outlined overleaf. Fill
in the stencilled shapes
using the No. 4 brush.

PAINTING·YOUR·TEAPOT·

1

Fill in your teapot stencil using the No. 6 artist's brush and white acrylic or emulsion paint. One coat should be sufficient.

2

Paint in the lines around the lid, spout and handle using the No. 1 artist's brush and black paint. This will help to give the teapot its rotund shape.

3

Using the pencil, lightly sketch the design onto the teapot. The hearts and added decor do not need to be precise distances from each other.

4

When you are happy with the proportions of the decorations, paint them in using the blue paint and No. 4 artist's brush.

5

Carefully shade and highlight the teapot following the instructions and tips on pages 12–13. Pay particular attention to the areas around the spout and handles. Add a little highlight to the teapot's knob.

DECORATING THE LID

Pencil in the design, paint in white and then add decorative details in blue.

5 *Painting a contrasting line around the edges of the hearts will help them to complement the teapot colours. Place dots around the rim of the lid.*

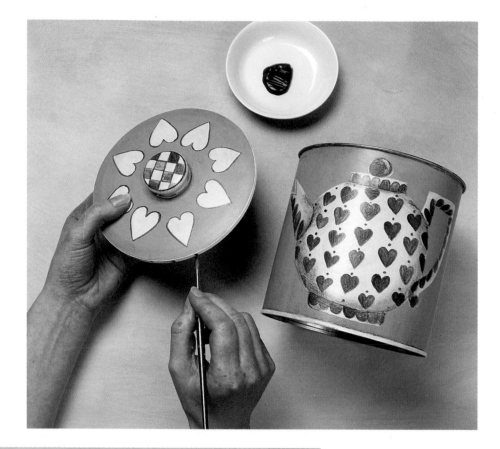

6 *Finish this project with antiquing liquid and polyurethane satin or gloss varnish (see page 10 for further information).*

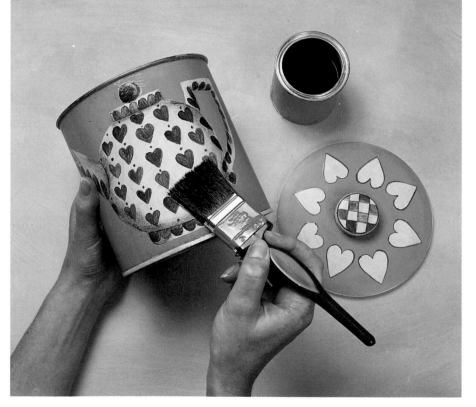

ALTERNATIVE TEAPOTS

Once you have your basic teapot shape, you can use that as a canvas and paint onto it any number of designs or patterns, either simple or complex. One possibility is to combine the teapot design with another of the projects featured in this book. For example, you could paint your basic teapot in a colour other than white and paint onto it a cockerel or auricula (you can always have your trace-off motif reduced to fit your teapot shape). The illustration shows one teapot that has been decorated in this way, combining the cockerel with different borders.

The teapot above features the cockerel from pages 38–47 and also makes great play of combining borders of many different styles.

The delicate dove motif from pages 78–87 forms the central image on the teapot below, which has been given an antique finish.

TRACE-OFF MOTIFS

The trace-off motifs given on these pages (118–26) are for each of the projects in this book. For information on using the motifs to make stencils and templates, and sizing them to fit your project, see pages 14–15. Some of the animals, such as the cockerels on page 120 and sheep on pages 122–3, have a variety of positions from which you can select your favourite.

TOPIARY TREES

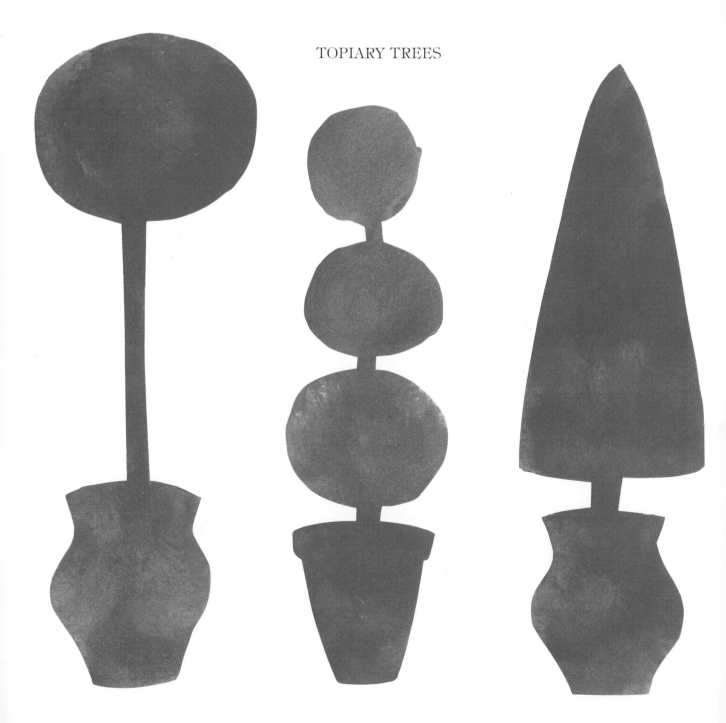

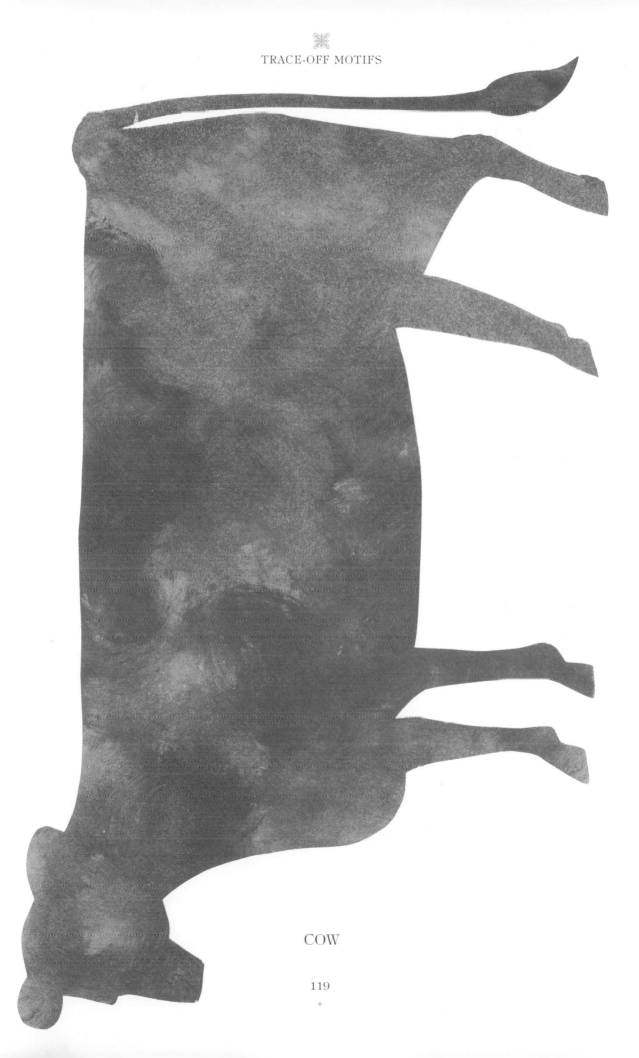

COW

119

COCKERELS

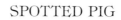

SPOTTED PIG

SHAGGY SHEEP

❋

TRACE-OFF MOTIFS

SHAGGY SHEEP

LEMONS AND PEARS

POT

GOOSE WITH A TARTAN BOW TIE

CHINA TEAPOT

DOVE OF PEACE

LIST OF SUPPLIERS

When I first began painting I was often frustrated by the lack of specialist products available in my area. This actually worked to my advantage in the long term as I learnt to improvise and use basic products that were readily available. Thus, although manufacturers do not recommend using water-based paints on top of oil-based paints, this is my normal way of painting. The majority of materials and equipment used in this book are available from most hardware and DIY stores.

PAINTS

Mid-sheen oil-based paints and emulsion paints are available at most large hardware and DIY stores in a wide range of colours. For decorative paints your local artists' supply store will normally carry a full range of acrylic paint colours in tubes. Some useful paint suppliers are:

Heritage Village Colours
UK
Heart of the Country
Home Farm
Swinfen
Nr Lichfield
Staffordshire WS14 9QR
Tel: 01543 481612
USA
Griffin Company Inc.
3501 Richmond Street
Philadelphia
PA 19134
Tel: 215 426 5976

Fired Earth
Fulham Road
117–119 Fulham Road
London SW3 6R4
Tel: 0171 589 0489

Laura Ashley
For information on your nearest stockists telephone:
UK
Mail Order and Customer Services
Tel: 01686 622116
USA
Mail Order and Customer Services
Tel: 617 457 6491

Dulux Decorative Paints
For details of product range and your nearest stockist contact the following:

UK
ICI Paints
Wexham Road
Slough
Berkshire SL2 5DS
Tel: 01753 550000
USA
ICI Paints
The Glidden Co.
925 Euclid Avenue
Cleveland
Ohio
0844115-1487
Tel: 216 344 8000
Canada
ICI Paints (Canada) Inc.
8200 Keele Street
Concord
Ontario
L4K 2A5
Tel: 905 669 1020

Folk Art Acrylic Paints
W. William & Son Bread Street Ltd
Regent House
1 Thane Villas
London N7 7PH
Tel: 0171 263

SUNDRY ITEMS

Papers & Paints
4 Park Walk
London SW10 0AD
Tel: 0171 352 8676
Large range of specialist paints plus brushes, pigments and varnishes

Green & Stone
259 Kings Road
London SW3 5ER
Tel: 0171 352 0837
Paints, artist's materials, specialist brushes, stencilling materials

Pine Brush Products
Stockingate
Coton Clanfield
Stafford ST18 9PB
Tel: 01785 282 799
Paints and specialist brushes

ITEMS TO PAINT

Ikea
UK
Brent Park Store
2 Drury Way
North Circular Road
Neasden
London NW10 0TH
Tel: 0181 208 5600
USA
Ikea Elizabeth
1000 Center Drive
Elizabeth
New Jersey 07202
Tel: 908 352 1550

Somerset Creative Products
Laurel Farm
Westham
Wedmore
Somerset BS2 84U
Tel: 01934 712 416
A range of white wooden items

Belinda Ballantine
The Old Bear House
53 High Street
Malmesbury
Wiltshire SN16 9AG
A selection of white wooden items

INDEX